My Talking Dictionary

& interactive cd rom

Scottish Gaelic & English

First published in 2005 by Mantra Lingua
Global House, 303 Ballards Lane, London N12 8NP
www.mantralingua.com

With thanks to the illustrators:
David Anstey, Dixie Bedford-Stockwell, Louise Daykin,
Alison Hopkins, Richard Johnson, Allan Jones,
Priscilla Lamont, Yokococo

A CIP record for this book is available from the British Library.

Contents

Clàr-innse

Mì Fhèin
Myself   page 4-5

Aodach
Clothes   page 6-7

An Teaghlach
Family   page 8

An Taigh
Home   page 9

An Taigh 's
na th' ann
House and   page 10-11
Contents

Measan
Fruit   page 12-13

Lusan
Vegetables   page 14-15

Biadh is Deoch
Food and Drink   page 16-17

An t-Àm-bìdh
Meal Time   page 18-19

Am Baile
Town   page 20-21

An t-Sràid Àrd
High Street   page 22-23

Sàbhailteachd
an Rathaid
Road Safety   page 24-25

Comhdhail
Transport   page 26-27

Beathaichean
Farm Animals   page 28-29

Ainmhidhean
Wild Animals   page 30-31

An Cladach
Seaside   page 32-33

An Raon-cluiche
Playground   page 34-35

An Seòmar-teagaisg
Classroom   page 36-37

Am Baga-sgoile
School Bag   page 38-39

Coimpiutairean
Computers   page 40-41

Comhdaichean-meallta
Dressing Up   page 42-43

Dèideagan is
Cleasan
Toys and Games   page 44-45

Spòrs
Sport   page 46-47

Ceòl
Music   page 48-49

Am Fànas
Space   page 50-51

An Aimsir
Weather   page 52-53

Mìosan na
Bliadhna
Months of   page 54
the Year

Ràithean
Seasons   page 54

Làithean na
Seachdaine
Days of the Week page 55

Ag Innse na
h-Uarach
Telling the Time   page 55

Dathan
Colours   page 56

Cruthan
Shapes   page 56

Àireamhan 1-20
Numbers 1-20   page 57

Faclan Calg-dhìreach
an Aghaidh
Opposites   page 58-59

Clàr-amais
Index   page 60-64

Myself

sùilean
eyes

falt
hair

beul
mouth

cluasan
ears

fiaclan
teeth

làmh
hand

òrdag
thumb

caol an dùirn
wrist

corragan
fingers

meadhan
waist

casan
feet

meòir
toes

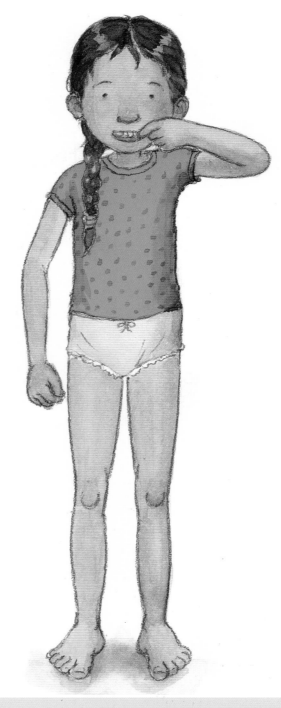

tha mi toilichte
happy

tha bròn orm
sad

tha fearg orm
angry

tha farmad agam
jealous

tha mi air bhiod
excited

Mì Fhèin

aodann
face

ceann
head

sròn
nose

amhach
neck

gàirdean
arm

gualainn
shoulders

goile
stomach

uileann
elbow

glùn
knee

druim
back

adhbran
ankle

cas
leg

tha mi gu bochd
sick

tha an t-acras orm
hungry

tha an t-eagal orm
scared

tha mi diùid
shy

tha mi sgìth
tired

Clothes

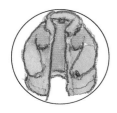 còta
coat

 sgarfa
scarf

 lèine-T
t-shirt

 dreasa
dress

 sgiort
skirt

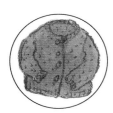 càrdagan
cardigan

 deise-shnàmh
swimming
costume

 stocainnean-
bodhaig
tights

 drathars
knickers

 brògan
shoes

Aodach

miotagan
gloves

ad
hat

lèine
shirt

geansaidh
jumper

briogais
trousers

briogais ghoirid
shorts

briogais-shnàmh
swimming
trunks

stocainnean
socks

fo-bhriogais
underpants

trèanairean
trainers

Family

seanmhair
grandmother

seanair
grandfather

seanair
grandfather

seanmhair
grandmother

piuthar athar
aunt

athair
father

màthair
mother

bràthair màthar
uncle

bràthair
brother

piuthar
sister

mac
son

nighean
daughter

leanbh
baby

Home
An Taigh

mullach-taighe
roof

seòmar-mullaich
attic

uinneag
window

seòmar-
ionnlaid
bathroom

seòmar-leapa
bedroom

seòmar-bìdh
dining room

cidsin
kitchen

trannsa
hallway

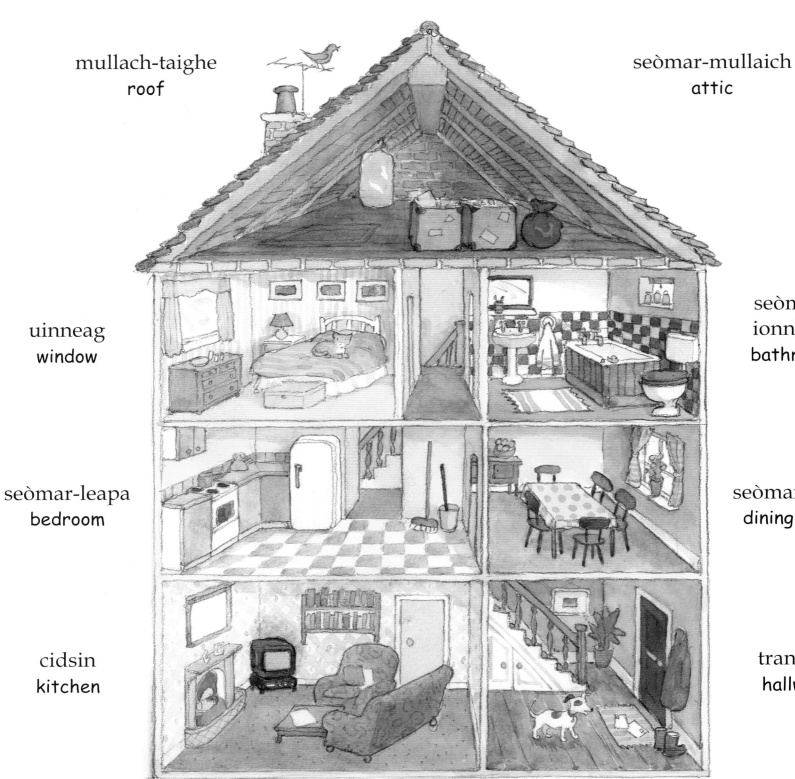

balla
wall

seòmar-suidhe
lounge/living room

staidhre
staircase

doras
door

House and Contents

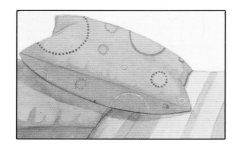
cluasag
pillow

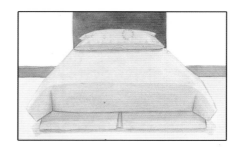
leabaidh
bed

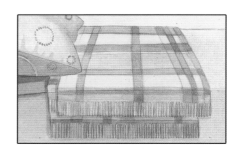
plaide
blanket

bine
bin

gaotharan
fan

lampa
lamp

fòn
telephone

inneal-
nigheadaireachd
washing machine

tostair
toaster

coire
kettle

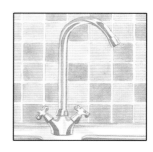
goc
tap

fuaradair
fridge

cucar
cooker

sinc
sink

An Taigh 's na th' ann

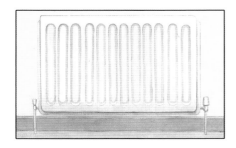

rèididheatar
radiator

amar
bath

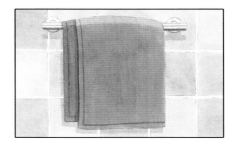

tubhailt
towel

sgàthan
mirror

taigh-beag
toilet

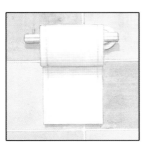

rola-toileit
toilet roll

frasair
shower

telebhisean
television

rèidio
radio

cùirtearan
curtains

preas
cupboard

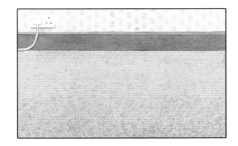

brat-ùrlair
carpet

langasaid
sofa

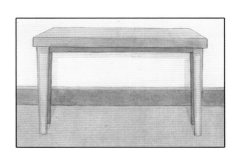

bòrd
table

Fruit

 banana
banana

 papaya
papaya

 peur
pear

 meal-bhuc
melon

 plumas
plum

 liomaid
lemon

 sirisean
cherries

 subhagan-làir
strawberries

12

Measan

fìon-dearcan
grapes

ubhal-giuthais
pineapple

mango
mango

orainsear
orange

peitseag
peach

ubhal
apple

laidhtidhean
lychees

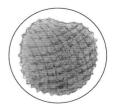

gràn-ubhal
pomegranate

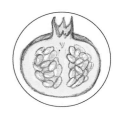

13

Vegetables

 uinnean
onion

 càl-colaig
cauliflower

 buntàta
potato

 coirce-milis
sweetcorn

 balgan-buacharach
mushroom

 tomàto
tomato

 pònairean
beans

 meacan dearg
radish

Lusan

gairleag
garlic

peapag
pumpkin/squash

cularan
cucumber

brocail
broccoli

piobar milis
pepper/capsicum

curran dearg
carrot

leiteas
lettuce

peasairean
peas

Food and Drink

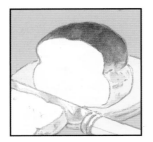

aran
bread

ìm
butter

silidh
jam

ceapaire
sandwich

siùcar
sugar

mìl
honey

gràn bracaist
cereal

bainne
milk

nùdailean
noodles

rìs
rice

spaghetti
spaghetti

pizza
pizza

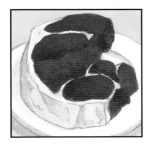

feòil
meat

iasg
fish

ubh
egg

càis
cheese

Biadh is Deoch

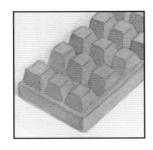

seaclaid
chocolate

siùcairean
sweets

cèic
cake

marag
pudding

iogart
yoghurt

reòiteag
ice cream

briosgaid
biscuit

brisgeagan
crisps

sliseagan
chips

ceitseap
ketchup

mustard
mustard

brot
soup

sùbh-measa
fruit juice

uisge mèinnearach
mineral water

salann
salt

piobar
pepper

Meal Time

 sgian
knife

 forc
fork

 spàin
spoon

 biorain-ithe
chopsticks

 muga
mug

 cupa
cup

 gloine
glass

An t-Àm-bìdh

truinnsear
plate

bobhla
bowl

pana
saucepan

wok
wok

aghann
frying pan

searrag
flask

bucas-lòin
lunchbox

Town

mòr-bhùth
supermarket

pàirc-chàraichean
car park

ionad-spòrs
sports centre

leabharlann
library

stèisean-poilis
police station

stèisean-thrèanaichean
train station

stèisean-smàlaidh
fire station

Am Baile

ospadal
hospital

pàirc
park

taigh-dealbh
cinema

garaids
garage

stèisean-bhusaichean
bus station

bùithtean
shops/stores

sgoil
school

High Street

taigh-bìdh
restaurant

flùranaiche
florist

bùth phàipearan-
naidheachd
newspaper stand

bùth-leabhraichean
book shop

feòladair
butcher

oifis a' phuist
post office

ceannaiche-èisg
fishmonger

ceannaiche-glasraich
greengrocer

ceimigear
chemist

fuineadair
bakery

banca
bank

bùth nan dèideagan
toyshop

bùth-cofaidh
coffee shop

gruagaire
hairdressers

Road Safety

rathad
road

solas-rathaid
traffic light

fear dearg
red man

fear uaine
green man

solais
lights

dealradair
reflector

clogaid baidhseagail
cycle helmet

crasgan-choisichean
pedestrian crossing

24

Sàbhailteachd an Rathaid

coisich
go

stad ort
stop

seall
look

èist
listen

clann a' dol thairis
children crossing

oifigear
cuairteachadh
crasgain-sgoile
school crossing patrol officer

crios-suidheachain
seat belt

cabhsair
pavement

Transport

itealan
aeroplane

laraidh
lorry/truck

càr
car

coidse
coach

bàta
boat

baidhsagail
bicycle

trèan
train

Comhdhail

motar-baidhg
motorbike

heileacoptair
helicopter

bus
bus

trama
tram

carabhan
caravan

long
ship

ricsea
rickshaw

Farm Animals

eun
bird

each
horse

tunnag
duck

cat
cat

gobhar
goat

coinean
rabbit

sionnach
fox

Beathaichean

bò
cow

cù
dog

caora
sheep

luch
mouse

cearc
hen

asal
donkey

gèadh
goose

Wild Animals

 muncaidh
monkey

 ailbhean
elephant

 nàthair
snake

 sìobra
zebra

 leòmhann
lion

 each-uisge
hippopotamus

 leumadair-mara
dolphin

 muc-mhara
whale

Ainmhidhean

panda
panda bear

sioraf
giraffe

càmhal
camel

tìgeir
tiger

mathan
bear

ceann-fionn
penguin

crogall
crocodile

cearban
shark

Seaside

muir
sea

tuinn
waves

tràigh
beach

freiceadan-snàimh
lifeguard

ola-grèine
sun lotion

sligean
shells

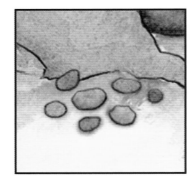

balbhagan
pebbles

feamainn
seaweed

An Cladach

pollag carraige
rock pool

crùbag
crab

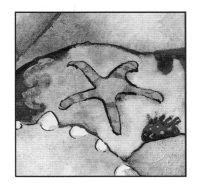

crosgag
starfish

seithear-pasgaidh
deckchair

gainmheach
sand

caisteal-gainmhich
sandcastle

bucaid
bucket

spaid
spade

Playground

dreallag
swing

timcheallan
roundabout

iobalag-obalag
seesaw

sloc-gainmhich
sandpit

tunail
tunnel

a-staigh/a-steach
in

a-muigh/a-mach
out

geàrr sùrdag
skip

framadh-dìridh
climbing frame

suas/a-nìos
up

sleamhnag
slide

sìos/a-nuas
down

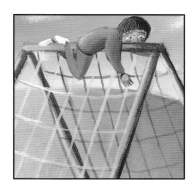

os cionn
over

fo
under

air beulaibh
in front

air cùlaibh
behind

The Classroom

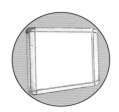 clàr-geal
white board

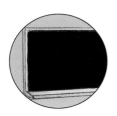 clàr-dubh
chalk board

 deasg
desk

 seithear
chair

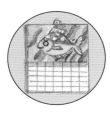 mìosachan
calendar

 clàradair-teip
tape recorder

 clàr-teip
cassette tape

 àireamhair
calculator

An Seòmar-teagaisg

tìdsear
teacher

leabhraichean
books

pàipear
paper

peant
paint

bruis-pheantaidh
paintbrush

siosar
scissors

glaodh
glue

teip steigeach
sticky tape

School Bag

 leabhar-sgrìobhaidh
writing book

 leabhar-matamataig
maths book

 pasgan
folder

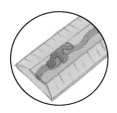 rùilear
ruler

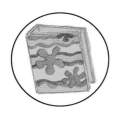 protractair
protractor

 peansail
pencil

 bioraiche peansail
pencil sharpener

Am Baga-sgoile

leabhar-leughaidh
reading book

creidhean
crayon

sreang
string

airgead
money

combaist
compass

rubair
rubber/eraser

peann-peilleig
felt tip pen

Computers

 lèirsinneir
scanner

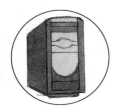 coimpiutair
computer

 follaisear
monitor

 meur-chlàr
keyboard

 luchag
mouse

 brat luchaig
mouse mat

Coimpiutairean

clò-bhualadair
printer

sgàilean
screen

eadar-lìon
internet

post-dealain
email

clàr cd
cd disc

clàr-bog
floppy disc

Dressing Up

speuradair
astronaut

poileas
police person

lighiche-sprèidh
vet

neach-smàlaidh
firefighter

neach-ealain
artist

ceannaiche
shop keeper

each-laoch
jockey

gille-cruidh
cowboy

còcaire
chef

Comhdaichean-meallta

banaltram
nurse

meacanaig
mechanic

draibhear-trèin
train driver

dannsair-ballet
ballet dancer

reultag-pop
pop star

tuaistear
clown

spùinneadair-mara
pirate

draoidh
wizard

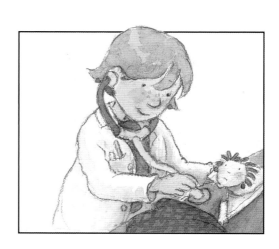

dotair
doctor

Toys and Games

balùn
balloon

grìogagan
beads

geama-bùird
board game

doileag
doll

taigh-doileig
doll's house

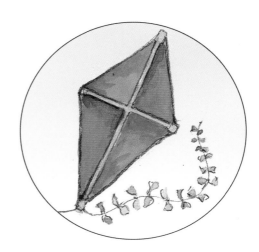

itealag
kite

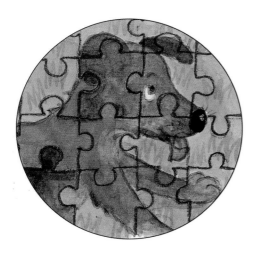

mìrean-measgaichte
puzzle

ròpa-sùrdaig
skipping rope

dòtaman
spinning top

Dèideagan is Cleasan

blocaichean-togail
building blocks

tàileasg
chess

dìsnean
dice

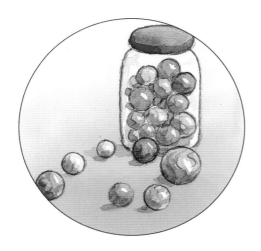

mirleagan
marbles

cairtean-cluich
playing cards

neach-brèige
puppet

teadaidh
teddy bear

meanbh-thrèan
train set

càr-cluich
toy car

Sport

ball-basgaid
basketball

ball
ball

criogaid
cricket

badmantan
badminton

snàmh
swimming

spèileadairean-rola
roller skates

racaid
racquet

spèileadairean-deigh
ice skates

teanas
tennis

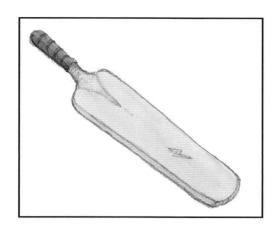

bata
bat

ball-lìn
netball

ball-coise
football

falbh air a' bhaidhsagail
cycling

rugbaidh
rugby

spèileabord
skateboard

hocaidh
hockey

Music

druma
drum

tabla
tabla

clàirneid
clarinet

duiseal
flute

clàrsach
harp

meur-chlàr
keyboard

giotar
guitar

taic-chiùil
music stand

Ceòl

triantan ciùil
musical triangle

trombaid
trumpet

maracannan
maracas

gan-gan
gan gan

piana
piano

cusail-bhinn
recorder

fidheall
violin

saidhleafon
xylophone

Space

A' Ghrian
sun

Mearcar
Mercury

Bhèanas
Venus

An Talmhainn
Earth

A' Ghealaich
moon

soitheach-fànais
spaceship

rionnag an earbaill
shooting star

rocaid
rocket

Am Fànas

Mars
Mars

Iùpatar
Jupiter

Satarn
Saturn

Ùranas
Uranus

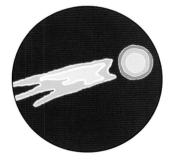

sgeith-rionnag
comet

rionnagan
stars

Neaptan
Neptune

Plùto
Pluto

51

Weather

tha a' ghrian ann
sunny

bogha-froise
rainbow

tha an t-uisge ann
rainy

tàirneanach
thunder

dealanach
lightning

tha gailleann ann
stormy

An Aimsir

tha gaoth ann
windy

tha ceò ann
foggy

tha sneachd ann
snowy

tha sgòthan ann
cloudy

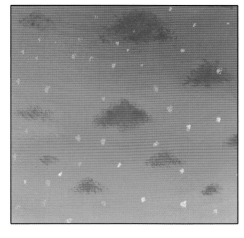

clachan-meallain
hail

tha reòthadh ann
icy

Months of the Year

Mìosan na Bliadhna

 Am Faoilleach
January

 An Gearran
February

 Am Màrt
March

 An Giblean
April

 An Cèitean
May

 An t-Ògmhios
June

 An t-Iuchar
July

 An Lùnastal
August

 An t-Sultain
September

 An Damhair
October

 An t-Samhain
November

 An Dubhlachd
December

Seasons

Ràithean

Earrach
Spring

Samhradh
Summer

Foghar
Autumn/Fall

Geamhradh
Winter

Monsun
Monsoon

Days of the Week   Làithean na Seachdaine

Diluain
Monday

Dimàirt
Tuesday

Diciadaoin
Wednesday

Diardaoin
Thursday

Dihaoine
Friday

Disathairne
Saturday

Didòmhnaich
Sunday

Telling the Time   Ag Innse na h-Uarach

cleoc
clock

latha
day

oidhche
night

madainn
morning

feasgar
evening

uaireadair
watch

cairteal as
dèidh
quarter past

leth-uair as
dèidh
half past

cairteal gu
quarter to

Colours

Dathan

dearg
red

orains
orange

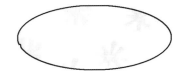

buidhe
yellow

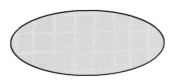

uaine
green

dubh
black

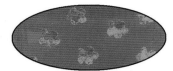

geal
white

glas
grey

gorm
blue

purpaidh
purple

pinc
pink

donn
brown

Shapes

Cruthan

cearcall
circle

rionnag
star

triantan
triangle

ugh-chruth
oval

còn
cone

ceart-cheàrnan
rectangle

ceàrnag
square

Numbers 1-20

Àireamhan 1-20

 1 a h-aon
one

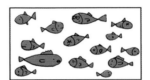 11 a h-aon deug
eleven

 2 a dhà
two

 12 a dhà dheug
twelve

 3 a trì
three

 13 a trì deug
thirteen

 4 a ceithir
four

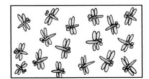 14 a ceithir deug
fourteen

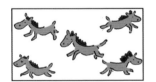 5 a còig
five

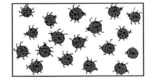 15 a còig deug
fifteen

 6 a sia
six

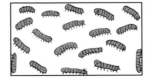 16 a sia deug
sixteen

 7 a seachd
seven

 17 a seachd deug
seventeen

 8 a h-ochd
eight

18 a h-ochd deug
eighteen

9 a naoi
nine

19 a naoi deug
nineteen

10 a deich
ten

20 fichead
twenty

Opposites

luath
fast

mall
slow

fosgailte
open

dùinte
closed

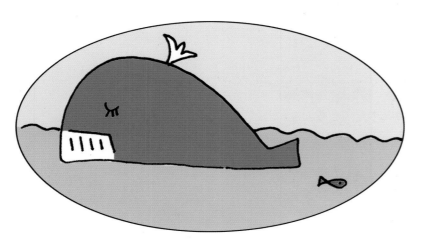

mòr
large

beag
small

fliuch
wet

tioram
dry

teth
hot

fuar
cold

milis
sweet

searbh
sour

Faclan Calg-dhìreach an Aghaidh

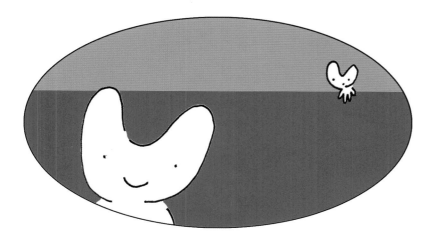

faisg
near

fad air falbh
far

clì
left

deis
right

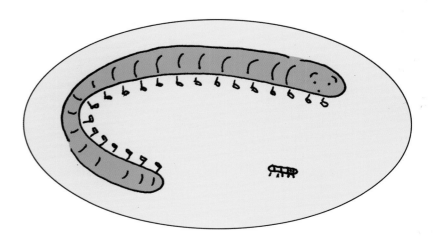

beulaibh
front

cùlaibh
back

fada
long

goirid
short

trom
heavy

eutrom
light

falamh
empty

làn
full

Index

Search for a word by picture or by the English word

Classroom
Page 36-37

 books

 calculator

 calendar

 cassette/tape

 chair

 chalk board

 desk

 glue

 paint

 paintbrush

 paper

 scissors

 sticky tape

tape recorder

 teacher

 white board

Clothes
Page 6-7

 cardigan

 coat

 dress

 gloves

 hat

 jumper

 knickers

 scarf

 shirt

 shoes

 shorts

 skirt

 socks

swimming costume

swimming trunks

 t-shirt

 tights

 trainers

 trousers

 underpants

Colours
Page 56

 black

 blue

 brown

 green

 grey

orange

 pink

 purple

 red

 white

 yellow

Computers
Page 40-41

 cd disc

 computer

 email

 floppy disc

 internet

keyboard

 monitor

mouse

mouse mat

 printer

 scanner

screen

Days of the Week
Page 55

 Monday

 Tuesday

 Wednesday

 Thursday

 Friday

Saturday

 Sunday

Dressing Up
Page 42-43

 artist

astronaut

ballet dancer

 car mechanic

 chef

 clown

 cowboy

 doctor

 firefighter

 jockey

 nurse

 pirate

 police person

 pop star

shop keeper

train driver

vet

wizard

Family
Page 8

 aunt

 baby

 brother

 daughter

 father

 grandfather

 grandmother

 mother

 sister

 son

 uncle

Farm Animals
Page 28-29

 bird

 cat

cow	cereal	pepper	lychees	coffee shop	lounge	lamp
dog	cheese	pizza	mango	fishmonger	roof	mirror
donkey	chips	pudding	melon	flower shop	staircase	pillow
duck	chocolate	rice	orange	greengrocer	wall	radiator
fox	crisps	salt	papaya	hairdressers	window	radio
goat	egg	sandwich	peach	newspaper stand	**House & Contents** Page 10-11	shower
goose	fish	soup	pear	post office	bath	sink
hen	fruit juice	spaghetti	pineapple	restaurant	bed	sofa
horse	honey	sugar	plum	toy shop	bin	table
mouse	ice cream	sweets	pomegranate	**Home** Page 9	blanket	tap
rabbit	jam	yoghurt	strawberries	attic	carpet	telephone
sheep	ketchup	**Fruit** Page 12-13	**High Street** Page 22-23	bathroom	cooker	television
Food & Drink Page 16-17	meat	apple	bakery	bedroom	cupboard	toaster
biscuit	milk	banana	bank	dining room	curtains	toilet
bread	mineral water	cherries	bookshop	door	fan	toilet roll
butter	mustard	grapes	butcher	hallway	fridge	towel
cake	noodles	lemon	chemist	kitchen	kettle	washing machine

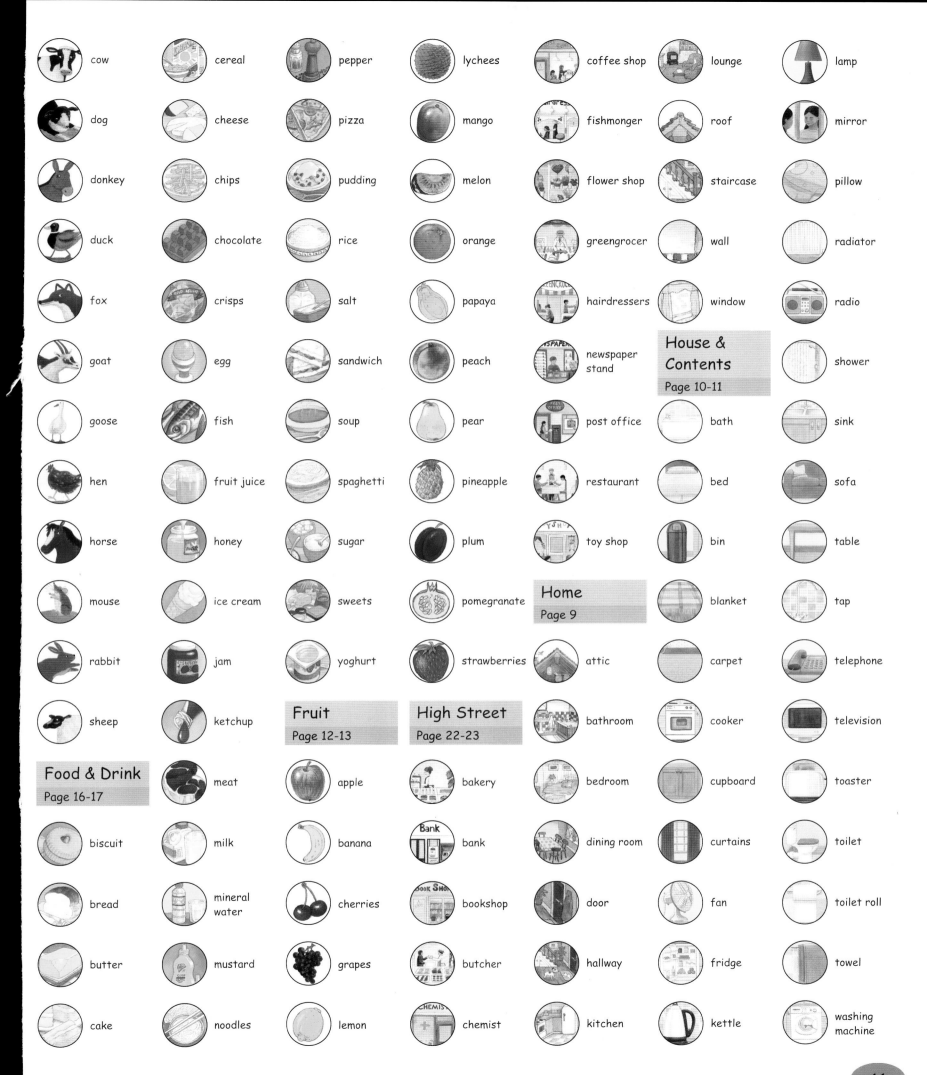

61

Meal Time
Page 18-19

 bowl

 chopsticks

 cup

 flask

 fork

 frying pan

 glass

 knife

 lunchbox

 mug

 plate

 saucepan

spoon

wok

Months of the Year
Page 54

 January

 February

 March

 April

 May

 June

 July

 August

 September

 October

 November

 December

Music
Page 48-49

 clarinet

 drum

 flute

 gan gan

 guitar

harp

keyboard

maracas

musical triangle

music stand

piano

recorder

tabla

trumpet

violin

xylophone

Myself
Page 4-5

 angry

 ankle

 arm

 back

 ears

 elbow

 excited

 eyes

 face

 feet

 fingers

 hair

hand

happy

head

hungry

jealous

knee

leg

mouth

neck

nose

Numbers 1-20
Page 57

 sad

 scared

 shoulders

 shy

 sick

 stomach

 teeth

 thumb

 tired

 toes

waist

wrist

one

two

three

four

Opposites
Page 58-59

 five

 six

 seven

 eight

 nine

 ten

 eleven

 twelve

 thirteen

 fourteen

 fifteen

sixteen

seventeen

eighteen

nineteen

twenty

 back

 closed

 cold

 dry

 empty

 far

 fast

 front

 full

 heavy

hot

large

left

light

long

near

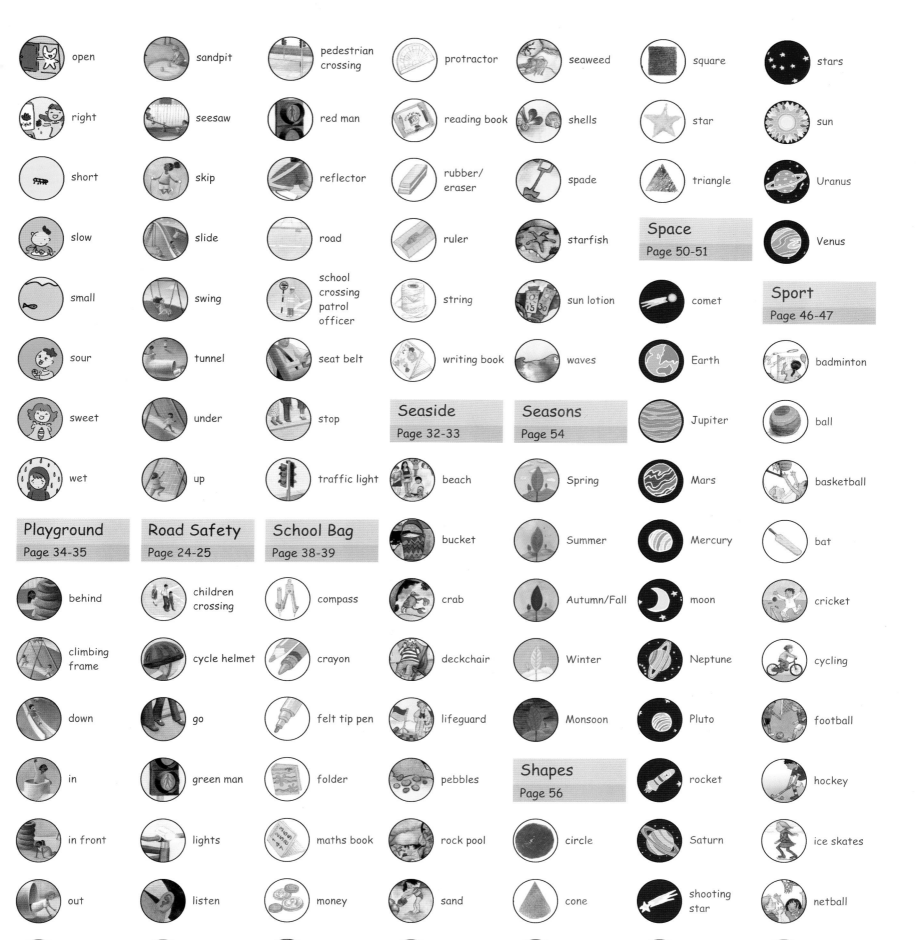

open	sandpit	pedestrian crossing	protractor	seaweed	square	stars
right	seesaw	red man	reading book	shells	star	sun
short	skip	reflector	rubber/eraser	spade	triangle	Uranus
slow	slide	road	ruler	starfish	**Space** Page 50-51	Venus
small	swing	school crossing patrol officer	string	sun lotion	comet	**Sport** Page 46-47
sour	tunnel	seat belt	writing book	waves	Earth	badminton
sweet	under	stop	**Seaside** Page 32-33	**Seasons** Page 54	Jupiter	ball
wet	up	traffic light	beach	Spring	Mars	basketball

Playground Page 34-35 | **Road Safety** Page 24-25 | **School Bag** Page 38-39

behind	children crossing	compass	crab	Summer	Mercury	bat
climbing frame	cycle helmet	crayon	deckchair	Autumn/Fall	moon	cricket
down	go	felt tip pen	lifeguard	Winter	Neptune	cycling
in	green man	folder	pebbles	Monsoon	Pluto	football
in front	lights	maths book	rock pool	**Shapes** Page 56	rocket	hockey
out	listen	money	sand	circle	Saturn	ice skates
over	look	pencil	sandcastle	cone	shooting star	netball
roundabout	pavement	pencil sharpener	sea	oval	Solar system	racquet
				rectangle	spaceship	roller skates

63

rugby

 skateboard

 swimming

 tennis

Telling the Time
Page 55

 clock

 day

 evening

 half past

 morning

 night

 quarter past

 quarter to

 watch

Town
Page 20-21

 bus station

 car park

 cinema

 fire station

 garage

 hospital

library
 library

 park

 police station

 school

 shops/ stores

 sports centre

 supermarket

 train station

Toys and Games
Page 44-45

 balloon

 beads

 board game

 chess

 dice

 doll

 doll's house

 kite

 marbles

 playing cards

 puppet

 puzzle

 skipping rope

 spinning top

 teddy bear

 train set

 toy car

Transport
Page 26-27

 aeroplane

 bicycle

 boat

 bus

 car

 caravan

 coach

 helicopter

 lorry/truck

 motorbike

 rickshaw

 ship

 train

 tram

Vegetables
Page 14-15

 beans

 broccoli

 carrot

 cauliflower

 cucumber

 garlic

 lettuce

 mushroom

 onion

 peas

 pepper/ capsicum

 potato

 pumpkin/ squash

 radish

 sweetcorn

 tomato

Weather
Page 52-53

 foggy

 hail

 icy

 lightning

 rainbow

 rainy

 snowy

 stormy

 sunny

 thunder

 windy

 cloudy

Wild Animals
Page 30-31

 bear

 crocodile

 dolphin

 elephant

 giraffe

 hippopotamus

 lion

 monkey

 panda bear

 penguin

 shark

 snake

 tiger

 whale

 camel

 zebra

building blocks